Heimlich's Manoeuvre

Acknowledgements

Versions of some of these poems first appeared in *A Dog Called Chance* (smith|doorstop, 1999) and in the following magazines and anthologies: *Poetry Ireland Review, Force 10, The North, FM magazine, The New Irish Poets, Bloodaxe* (ed Selina Guiness, 2004) *Magnetic North, Verbal Arts Centre* (ed John Brown, 2005). 'The Chief Radiographer Considers' won the 2011 Hippocrates Poetry Prize and was published in the Guardian. 'Gist' was commended in the 2011 Edwin Morgan International Poetry Prize. 'Fathom' was placed third in the 2013 Ballymaloe Poetry Prize.

I thank the Arts Council of Northern Ireland who have thrice granted awards, buying me time to write, and the Tyrone Guthrie Centre at Annaghmakerrig for productive, enriching and fattening residencies. A debt is due to my friends, Siobhan Hunter, Jean Bleakney, Brian Hollywood and John Brown who read and commented on early versions of these poems. Thanks also to the members and facilitators of the writers' group at Queen's University Belfast which I have attended sporadically over many years, most especially Carol Rumens and Sinead Morrissey. More recently, for their great generosity, my gratitude to Ciaran Carson and the cohort of reader/writers who meet each week at the Seamus Heaney Centre at Queen's. Thanks also to Paul Maddern from whose bank of beautiful photographs I chose the cover image, to Malachi O'Doherty for making me laugh for the author photo, and to Paula Meehan, whose writing and example got me started.

Finally, to my stalwart friends and family. To the Hunters and Macdonalds who frequently mind the dog. And especially to my father, Jimmy, to whom I dedicate this work.

Heimlich's Manoeuvre

Paula Cunningham

smith|doorstop

Published 2013 by
Smith/Doorstop Books
The Poetry Business
Bank Street Arts
32-40 Bank Street
Sheffield S1 2DS
www.poetrybusiness.co.uk

ISBN 978-1-906613-83-9

British Library Cataloguing-in-Publication Data.
A catalogue record for this book is available from the
British Library.

Typeset by Utter
Printed by printondemand.com
Cover design by Utter
Cover image: Keel 3 by Paul Maddern
Author photo: Malachi O'Doherty

Smith/Doorstop Books is a member of Inpress,
www.inpressbooks.co.uk. Distributed by Central Books Ltd.,
99 Wallis Road, London E9 5LN.

The Poetry Business is an Arts Council
National Portfolio Organisation

Supported by
**ARTS COUNCIL
ENGLAND**

... This is a street
you can't step into twice ...
the unremembered, unredeemed,
ordinary, neither true nor false,
and unaccountable as love.

– Stuart Dybek

What did I know, what did I know
of love's austere and lonely offices?

– Robert Hayden

Contents

For my father,
Jimmy Cunningham

Finding the Well

My grandfather found the well
and attended the sick – a dowser
better known as 'The Doctor'.

At Lisfannon he bought the house
my uncle won in a poker game,
the first in a row of identical tardises

over the road from the strand.
Not the old man whose cure
for the lump on my hand was the threat

of a thump with a Bible, and worked,
but younger and leaner, pacing the field,
the twist and lurch of the rod

his gift that slaked six houses' throats;
at his desk or in homes
round Omagh and Carrickmore

between and after the wars,
when payment was often spuds or hay,
the odd poached pheasant or fish.

On the Shankill a patient presented
to me. Mr Lyons wore tweeds,
his accent rose west of the Bann:

Fermanagh, south Derry, Tyrone?
One of The Doctor's patients from Carrickmore,
come up in the fifties to join the R.U.C.

His last word on Grandpa: *he wasn't
a hard man to pay.* A big tin of Family Circle
appeared, at tea-break the following day.

Geography and Sweetshops

Lisfannon, Buncrana, Bunduff, Mullaghmore, Rossnowlagh.
The best places to swim were always over
the border. In the car killing time

we played *I spy with my little eye ...*
and *Spot the soldiers*, their camouflage
too dark for August grass

... something beginning with
h ... The wee white house, windows for eyes
one either side of the thick red line on the map.

We imagined the little old woman –
she was always little and old –
waking each morning in the

South and having eggs
for breakfast in the North
and maybe crossing again

to clean her teeth
and check her hair
in the big old bathroom mirror

in the South.
What accent would she use?
Did her cattle favour

Southern or Northern
grass? Where did they give good milk?
And where did her children

go to school and did they like to change
their accents too and did they ever
get confused?

❧

The sea and Southern bread, and sweets we couldn't get
at Auntie Maggie's shop. Skittles, Golden Crisp,
and *richer, smoother, creamy* Dairy Milk.

In the sweet-shop in Buncrana, women
smile at us and call us refugees. We learn
to use our strongest

Northern accents
and look sad. This guarantees
free sweets at the beginning.

❧

Back home, we never knew
when Auntie Maggie'd come to stay.
We knew to open the windows

when the siren went. We knew
if an inspector called that this
window or that door

hadn't been broken before.
We knew that Auntie Maggie's blood pressure
was bad and that it blew sky-high –

she'd get bloodshot eyes –
each time an unattended car
appeared outside the shop

but that mostly people forgot
and it was nothing,
a scare. And then it wasn't

and she'd come to stay
and her Maeve didn't eat gravy
and she didn't have to

and Auntie Maggie's boys could say bad words
and nothing happened
and they could eat sweets all the time

and she'd say nothing
and they were ruined.
And when the windows came in all the sweets

in the shop would be ruined too
and even the ones buried at the bottom
and even the ones in the store-room that didn't have

a window
would have to be destroyed
but we would have eaten them anyhow

and we could have cried
at the thought
of all that waste.

Cats – a Retrospective

I believe to have one dog is better
than a hundred thousand cats, I believe
whatever anybody older than me says

except my older sisters who know nothing
and our neighbours, the McDevitts,
who have far too many cats.

I believe what Mum and Dad,
my teachers and the priests
tell me is right and that,

believing them, I'll be right too.
I believe there's a right way of doing things,
I believe in the essential beauty

of the thing done right and in always,
always doing the right thing.
I believe that any job worth

doing is worth doing well,
I believe that God's a Catholic,
that he's everywhere, I believe

it will be twenty years
before I hear the thing
about the many ways

to skin a cat and I
believe that even then
I'll wonder which one's right.

Ceremony

In her third year at the Convent
my cousin Millie won a Prize
for scholarly activity –

didn't tell a sinner –
just rushed onto the stage
at Prizegiving, blushing

gave Sister Ignatius the name
of the girl who should
have won, skulked off again.

Nobody seemed to find it odd.
I was in first year. I thought
I would have liked a Prize.

Years later I win an award
and hide it in my knicker drawer
beside my Irish passport.

Mother's Pride

Handy with a knife,
his preferred medium
was Mothers Pride plain toast.
This is the way the nuns
eat – soldiers. This
is the Protestant half.

Here's Omagh, Belfast,
Enniskillen, Dublin, Donegal
with Errigal hastily moulded
from Clew Bay, a crumb
for an island for every day
of the year, and Cork,

where John Mac lives.
Lough Erne's two narrow slits;
Lough Neagh a slanty
oblong poked right through.
A final flourish, grinning,
his *pièce de resistance*

was the border
which my frowning mother
quickly buttered over,
stabbing the bread,
drawing the knife
out clean.

Banquet

O squat round Banquet
    margarine tub, your black
and blue *SUPERSOFT* letters,

on permanent Special:
    Sleek Sentinel, for weeks
you have held centre-stage.

Flanked by the HP sauce
    and the salt, you're one fifth
of the Kerrygold butter

we crave. Our throats
    burn gold with the blur
of the buttercup's disc.

We freeze when the yellowy
    ingot appears; it sweats
on its rose-spattered plate.

            ∾

O Banquet, Pale Champion
    Duller of Hunger, observe us now
shovelling butter.

It's not a bit of wonder
    it never lasts.

Hats

The year I tried on voices just like hats.

Whore hat
Bored hat
Life's-a-fucking-chore hat
Tore hat
Sore hat
Never-bloody-score hat
Can't-take-any-more hat
Roar hat
Soon-be-thirty-four hat.

I was running out of fabric

But then I found a blessed hat
Poetry-obsessed hat
Need-a-bloody-rest hat
Got-to-go-out-west hat
Realised that politics are best avoided
Put on my Sunday-best hat
Soon got bored with that.

Tried on my dead-serious-issues hat
My rhyme-all-the-time hat
My why-can't-I-write-like-Paula-Meehan hat
My fek-it-have-a-drink-and-write-like-Brendan-Behan hat.

The year I tried on voices just like hats
The weather changed
The ceasefires came
And screaming like a banshee
My severed tongue grew back.

My father wore a hat when I was little
we lived in Omagh O-M-A-G-Haitch or –Aitch
as tribally decreed. He was a travelling salesman
for ice-cream; a Dublin firm Hughes Brothers or H.B.
he was their Northern Ireland diplomat.

He knew his clients well – a studied discipline,
some would not buy HB ice-cream on principle.
My father'd done his homework;
to some he'd sell Haitch
B, to others Aitch B.

One day in Derry/Londonderry my father's car was hijacked.
The men wore hats pulled down with holes for eyes and mouth.
They held a gun, they nudged his hat.
They asked my father where we lived
and ordered him to spell it.

᷍

The year I tried on voices just like hats.

Fiction

Too many books spoil the
my mother her head in a cliff

again, searching for gannets' eggs
to assemble the blackcurrant soufflé

she swears had been served at her wedding,
my father making a show of licking the cream,

his glee as he needled the priest
with talk of their passionate life.

But you, she cried, *with your head in a book*
Look out or you'll scramble your eggs.

Changing Rooms

Have I told you how I
was the last in the class
to get one; how I was teased
for a year; how I knew
when I got one the teasing
would only get worse;
how I longed for and dreaded
it in equal measure.

My mother's whispered lie
she needs   a bra;
the Misses O'Reilly's dextrous eyes
sizing me up:
30 their damning verdict
A   A
cup.

From under the counter
little by little
five plain boxes
stacked and floating
flat on my upturned palms.

Our procession facing
the shuttered changing
room; my mother & Miss O'Reilly
hovering; the prickle of white
padded nylon, the deep pink rose
sewn on where the cleavage
should be. A pink fog
closing in, its crimson pall.

And did I ever tell you about my friend
who, furnished with a bra
in another town,
in a family of sisters,
never having seen one on the line,
wore her new bra for months
before her mother spotted it,
black on the bedroom floor?

Her mother, it transpired,
hung them at the back
of the airing cupboard.

The same friend's sister,
kissing a boy
and feeling his hand
flutter at her chest,
turns on the light
and puts her glasses on
to help him find
the thing he has mislaid.

My sister, her first son
at her breast, felt her shirt sodden
under one arm,

how she balked at the prospect
of underarm milk: an aberrant
nipple, common enough,

covert until called upon,
there in the bathroom mirror
true to type.

❧

And my friend's South American friend
who adopted a child
and bottle-fed
using a tube
which was fixed
to her nipple?

How after a couple of weeks
her milk came in.

(And how her breasts held sway
in the bedroom
hosing her husband
drenching the marriage bed.)

❧

My mother's mother
made a pact with cancer,
whose chop and change concession
cost her breast, returned
to the consulting room
and gravely pressed the surgeon
– lopsidedness felt loathsome –
to remove its blameless fellow;
how gamely he'd obliged.

And how she lived well
past her ninetieth year,
robust of bra
and girdled
to the last.

A Dog Called Chance

29 August 1998

I've jooked into a pub
to avoid the American woman
who's been shooting sheep and shopkeepers all week.

Inverness. I've seen
no monsters here.
The churches are deserted

but for tourists;
when the tall girl sang an Ave
for her boyfriend

– she hid behind a pillar –
it echoed so
I swore I heard an angel.

It's Saturday.
It's been two weeks.
A golden labrador's cavorting in the river

chasing gulls – the grey ones
& the fatter ones with brown spots,
scalloped edges in the pattern on their wings,

tails opening and closing like Chinese fans.
The dog's called Chance,
I swear, I asked its owner –

a great pink tent of a woman with kids –
she tells me that the brownish gulls are youngsters,
bigger than both their parents put together.

The woman with the cameras has gone –
I think I'll travel back first class –
I should be on the train by three,

asleep before Dunblane.
It's lovely here, I had
to get away.

I love the way they ask you
where you're staying,
meaning where you live

as if you have a choice.
I think again of leaving
till my face hurts

and I scrounge a cigarette.
In Irish the word for poem's
the word for gift.

Sometimes Dancing

Advance, retreat, the chandeliers
are hot tonight, their cut beads
bend the golden light like tears.

Advance, retreat, pass through, dance home.
Gallop. Swing with your partner. Change.
In her dream she is princess, pale

hair coiled in knots, she's trussed in whalebone,
small breasts thrust to touch the heavy choker
at her throat. Advance, retreat. She's been trained

for this, shoulders back, the particular
angle chin and throat describe, balancing
heavy books she thought were made

for practice, and later Mother's precious plates
from China. Sometimes, dancing, she'll force her eyes
up, back, till over the eyebrows' arch

she sees the golden drops, and the room
spins. She does not see the men
she dances with, though she feigns

attention, smiling. She feels
their hands long after they've passed on.
When she dances with Clara she holds tighter

than she should, pushes herself beyond
giddiness. Leans into her. A little.
Once in her dream, swinging,

their bodies locked together and they flew.
She woke to a crashing of plates, a tangle
of sheets in her narrow bed, the heart galloping.

The Question of Punctuation
... all I could see were question marks ...
– Sylvia Plath

when all I can see are question marks
my body craves a different punctuation
the continuity of commas
the implied motion of a semicolon
a syntax disrupted
by dashes or brackets
and later recovered
the colon's bold staccato

even the finality of a full
stop seems attractive when sometimes
all I can see are question marks
and I have to be restrained
from tearing up
the page

burning
the book

The Cloudhouse

The nameless dead dwell in a house
where walls drip choice and all
official documents dissolve.

From room to room they know
no need of doors; who tripped
and froze and shuffled here now glide.

Their cheeks are pink, their hair
is slick, they wear no clothes,
their laundry never dries.

Our nameless dead hold hands.
They claim the names they craved
but dared not win. On beaten feet

they voted with, they dance.
Night after night they're held;
they dream ensemble on giant waterbeds.

The nameless dead laugh often
in the cloudhouse. Their pills mildew
and rot beside the nameless dreads they've dropped;

their lips are moist, their brows
are kissed, they do not miss their lost
lives and are glad.

Notes from an Ear

I'm small enough to fit
into a teacup. You underestimate
me; this flesh means nothing

and mostly I keep
to myself. I love bone,
its occasional braille,

but mainly I cherish its smooth darkness.
I thrive on disturbance, I know
about waves, the way molecules

bounce and knock – slow,
fast. I abhor
vacuums. My centre is

all coil and deep canal.
Though I live for sound
and music is everything –

malleus
        incus
                stapes

– imbalance is the biggest part
of movement. Because of me
the deaf stand up and dance.

Losing the Keys

Losing the keys I'm at a loss again.
Though I lock myself out in all weathers,
it would appear I specialise in grey skies, rain.

Losing the keys or dreading losing them
it's all the same, the art of losing being
well-established in my head,

I set my mind on damage limitation, spares
planted in flowerbeds, lodged with friends; I don
bright Gore-Tex, carry an umbrella like a prayer.

But worse than being stranded on your own
doorstep in rain is getting in, no sweat, let's say
a sunny day, Chubbing the door, putting on

the chain, losing the keys inside the house:
sitting indoors outside yourself again.

Salvage

whole seasons
you're losing

what happens

is there
in Heaven

a roof-space

where you can
collect them

Bane

You're my ardent opponent at Scrabble,
    an athlete
        I've tried
                to outrun,
    the knots that you tie
            make me hobble and trip,
our acquaintance has seldom been fun.

You're a master at improvisation,
    my stand-in with tits
        and no tongue,
      you're calamity
         certain
to happen,
        my seductively chain-smoking gun.

You're a claw-and-tooth cat in my cradle,
    you're a dance
        at a crossroads
             that's mined,
    you're a pain you're my shame
        you're entirely to blame,
a relation I've longed to un-find.

But lately I'm inching toward   you,
    my succubus bastard
my twin,
  and I'm bound to attest
    that I'm loathing you
  less
as our three-legged shuffle begins.

The Chief Radiographer Considers

Pierre Curie, who was wont to carry radium
in his breast pocket, the red brand
on his chest which would never heal,

his femurs already aglow; and the dray horse
on the narrow Paris street beside Pont Neuf
that robbed the white-hot lesions of their prize.

He dreams the powder Marie kept at her bedside,
its pretty scintillation as she slept; her own death
from leukaemia, the damage accruing slowly like a debt,

the compound interest in the body's bank.
He imagines her fingertips scraping each page,
her notebooks, her letters, her cookbooks yes,

that seventy years from her death are housed in lead;
how researchers at the Bibliothèque Nationale
are required to sign a disclaimer.

He's surer of DNA, its ladder and its snakes,
how everything unravels and decays. He presses
the bright red button again, again.

Amalgam

I know eight hundred and sixty-seven people orally;
I ask them probing questions,
they open up to me.

They send a guinea-pig to test
my mettle and if I'm patient
make a good impression

they bring their friends and family;
their children and their granny
come, it's pleasant.

They open up to me.
I scrub and glove,
stand on my hands

and walk the wire with them.
Sometimes they bite and spit.
I mirror them, refract

that light, see past
their bones and skin.
I outsmart pain

I see them whole and will
them smile again. I iron
out their inconsistencies.

They open up to me.
Wider, wider, close your eyes
I then rip off my mask, extract

my fee. To compensate
I sugar them with pieces
plucked from me.

Too Dear

You said you'd phone me soon
I never thought to question you

Call me peak rate or never call

I said I'd trade a kiss for flowers
You said you'd do without

Call me peak rate or never call

At night you made my walls rebound
By day you could not spare a pound

Call me peak rate or never call

You took to calling once a week
On Sundays after six

Call me peak rate or never call

I realised the strings were false
I took my scissors from their box

Call me peak rate or never call

I cut the ties that did not bind
My dear, I was too dear for you

Call me peak rate or never call

Broken Couplets

Today we traded misery for sadness & I'm glad.
While misery begets despair I know that sorrow passes.

You trebled my self-confidence, together we destroyed it.
Now I needs must sow my own and owning it deploy it.   .

Debriefing we discover how our legacies are different:
While I remember tendernesses you'll recall positions.

As for the woman thrusting for your up-and-coming 'us'
I wish you well. I swear. I do. I wish the lady thrush.

Skin

Today my teenage godson
stretched cling-film over the
toilet bowl to repay the mother
who had pissed him off. He
quickly applies the film and
puts the lid back down. The
ends he smoothes along the
toilet's neck. My friend, his
mother, cops on right away.
(He never puts the seat down;
besides, the boy's ham-fisted,
and a wrinkle in the skin has
caught the light.) She peels
the film off but doesn't say.
She finds that she no longer
needs, no longer wants, to go.

My friend talks more than me;
she always has. She never even
touches her coffee till several
minutes after I've drained my
cup. She claims to like the
skin. She eases it back with
the back of her spoon and
sprinkles sugar in. A skin has
formed across the eager space
I cleared for you. While I have
been distracted, the cup has
somehow filled itself again.

Aubade

Bring the muse into the kitchen
— Walt Whitman

A man is squeezing oranges in my kitchen.
I am down the corridor in bed
and he is squeezing oranges
in my kitchen.
From where I lie
I cannot see the man
but I've deduced
that he
is squeezing oranges.

There is something tremendously erotic
about a man
squeezing oranges.
What is erotic is the sound.
This man
has found my orange squeezer
without my prompting.
He does not know I know
he's squeezing oranges.

Lying here, listening
to the sound of a man
secretly squeezing oranges
at 1.09 of a Sunday afternoon,
I am struck by the fact
that I've never heard any sound
quite so erotic
as the sound of a man
squeezing oranges.

Because

they do not usually borrow
your underwear &

there is nothing in the woman
that compares to the silk

of scalp over bone when the hair
leaves. This & the miracle

of stubble. There is
no equivalent either to returning

after a long day at the office, a day
sufficient to make you forget

the man who stayed,
& finding the loo-seat

up. The way their water
falls, louder & unmuffled,

akin sometimes to music
or children's laughter,

& the way they stand, their eyes
already far-off trancers

following the band. The household bill
for toilet roll decreases; feminine

hygiene costs are also down. Mostly
they earn more anyway, have better

motors & prefer to drive, improving
fuel economy. Sperm is also

a consideration. The way a ball
will fall quite unabashed

from their shorts
while the small amphibian

sleeps in its scratchy nest;
the way you always get

to read them first,
& Y-fronts

on the washing-line
the only flags

that ever
make you smile.

On Being the Least Feminist Woman You've Ever Met

Miguel, for instance:
when the man with the bicycle
and half a nose, (differential

diagnosis carcinoma, chancre – a long
shot – trauma, a bite, a diagonal slice
with a carving knife) a strawberry

in horizontal section, gestured
to me, I followed dust
through olive and orange groves

above Javea, not thinking,
then thinking, as he abandoned
his ancient bike against

the one stone wall, why
am I doing this,
but doing it nonetheless,

aping charades of ages,
stories, my made-up *marido*
and children, ten, seven,

three, back at the villa,
waiting for me, while I shifted
a band from my middle

to marriage finger,
how often I've performed
that small manoeuvre;

how the heft and scent
of oranges he plucked
to fill my rucksack staggered

me; how parting we came cheek
to nose to cheek; how
the octogenarian chancer

squeezed my ass; how I knew
I should have slapped
him; how the valley

offered us back
as we slapped ourselves;
how as we laughed and

laughed again, the gaps
between his teeth
were open gates.

How sweet the juice
I later, I assure you,
drank alone.

Seeing Things

At the Winter Park ski-holiday reunion
who swans in only Stevie
whose legs don't take him far –
he'd been tinkering under a car
when the bomb went off.

Answer: the skin.
It's Trivia night
and we're in with a chance.
All the other tables are offering liver.
What is the largest organ in the body?

In Winter Park we're triple-
wrapped in thermals
but he's shirtless:
a sophisticated instrument
of thermo-regulation.

Homoeostasis: the body
as a furnace;
the sweat-glands
and erector pili muscles
co-operate to keep the body cool.

The hypothalmus
is conductor of the body's
secret business;
but skin grafts don't have glands
and scars are bald.

Anyway Stevie has walked
the twenty yards from his special car
and he's wrecked
and his stumps are sore
and we get tore in to the drink

and we all get legless
and everyone in the Welly Bar
(we're only here for the ramps
and we've jumped the queue)
is legless and Stevie has taken his off,

all smooth American tan
with the socks and the cool shoes on,
and we laugh out loud
at the pretty woman
on stilts who almost

jumps out of her skin
and the plastered people
who swear
they're seeing things
and we know they are.

Seed

With every letter now I'll send you
unnamed seeds.
You will, behind the house,
hoe out some soil
and plant them
with bare hands.

You must remember them on dry days
with melt-water you'll carry from the river,
a little food (organic)
then just wait.

In time you'll see the earth
thrill at your touch, burst open
yawning multi-coloured flowers,
raucous beds of love.

Astronomy for Beginners

Bewitched by stars,
cool phosphorescence
at our feet, we wade knee-deep Atlantic,
August 3 a.m.

and later, finding one sweater still dry,
we sidle home, wearing it together,
suddenly Siamese, tripping, laughing,
taking turns at sleeves and carrying

our bundle of wet clothes,
the Plough our torch and guide,
with other constellations
we can't know

but promise to learn
by heart this side of Christmas.

Driving North

Returning late in rain from Connemara,
each time we pass a 'Welcome to our County'
I slow and sound the horn, a single toot,

Galway *toot* Mayo *toot* Sligo...
and I'm explaining 'Davy did this,
my first real boyfriend, twenty years ago.'

And when approaching sleep you call me sweetie,
I know your friend, your ex, still calls you that,
and later when you flex and click your knuckles

you will tell me of a lover, way back,
who'd twist and stretch so ardently
that each and every vertebra would crack.

And when you make me scratch
your back it's childhood and your daddy;
the wheaten bread each Saturday's my ma;

that thing when I touch the back
of your hand with the back of a hot
coffee spoon's a man I loved abysmally

and that man's granddad. And this is how it is:
angels and ogres jostle at our shoulders,
anxious for their chance to vanquish time,

and these fleeting appearances, *toot*, brief
visitations that make us scowl or smile, keep
all of our losses, even our dead, alive.

At First Our Letters

always crossed
(we couldn't wait)
they bulged in heavy

over air-mail rate,
envelopes tense
with offings.

I fancied them as birds
stilling their wings
to touch or kiss

mid-flight, larks maybe,
hell-bent on nesting,
locations we couldn't

ever agree, both
of us wanting it both
ways, native and

exotic – twigs, feathers
ferns in our mouths.
Where do we go

from here?
Your last letter burned
on my desk for days –

a thin affair.
I hesitate, a feather
in my throat. Weeks

pass; I still can't lift the pen
to shift the tense,
and every night I choke.

The Birds of Sri Lanka
December 2004

1. Colombo

By six a.m. the Galle Face Green's
a massive outdoor gym:
walls, park benches, railings

are props for presses, sit-ups,
long leg stretches; steps
are for stepping down and up

at speed, and tennis balls for agile
sleights of foot by skinny baseball-
hatted youths. The rank and file

do sprints and jerks, then squat
en masse to meditate, perform a stiff-
legged march, high-step, about turn,

stop. The men applaud their coach,
shake hands all round, fall out.
A woman breathes, faces the ocean,

her semaphore raising her dress;
an old man bends to praise the sun
two bone-thin dogs play dead in.

The company disperses.
By eight the foot of air above the green's
reclaimed by small swift birds.

2. Postcard

Cranes, egrets, kingfishers, pelicans, eagles,
blue-tailed bee-eaters (five in a row
on a wire) crows, many many crows.
Owls, herons, swifts or maybe
swallows, I never can tell. German birds,
English birds, Sri Lankan birds in saris
of many colours. Crows, more crows.
Bird in blue bikini still on beach
night falling xxx

3. There and Now

How floating one day I watched fish fly beside me
That I dived in the water when Fasmi put out the nets
Why most of the fishes we caught that morning were dead
How the catamarans over there are called oruvas
That I am a fish and my element is salt
When I couldn't get back how Aruna threw me a line
Why blue-tailed bee-eaters fly from the high Himalayas
That the geographical cure only partially works
How after the wave an eagle hung over the ocean
Though remembered kisses litter this city I live
That water still laps at the door of the room where I sleep
Where you are a catch in my throat a catch in my throat
That today I smiled at a man and he gave me a feather
Why I miss you most when really good things happen

4. Flight

a Prada handbag flagging
    her first-class status
a lone man sobbing loudly in Departures
    people with no bags
people with duty-free bags
    a woman in filthy teddy-bear pyjamas
her young son and daughter
    expressionless becalmed
a bloke in one Nike track-shoe
    and one sandal
people who wouldn't be seen dead
    holding hands holding hands

Fruit

From a forty-year blue
you appeared, more beautiful
than any of us, replete

with grace – the image of yourself:
no lily nor eagle nor serpent
nor dove; no bright flames

licking your feet; no shaft
of light relating you to Heaven.
In lieu of a scroll you proffer

the scrapbooks your mother
compiled: a childhood
looking like no-one.

꿍

Look at us now. Observe
how you stir us – root, branch
and leaf – blossom

and fruit upon fruit
making good
the tree.

Earthwish

after "Irisch" by Paul Celan

Grant me the wayleave
across the drawbridge to your sleep,
the by-your-leave
to wend the wild meanders of your dreams,
the privilege, now I'm fit, to split the turf
along your breast's incline
come dawn.

Gist

In this his apocryphal pre-incarnation I have him in nightgown and cap
clutching a candlestick, big Willie Winkie cack-handed with drink,
he soft-shoes, manoeuvres himself in behind her, just as the first of his hic-
cups erupts, impressing the spoon of himself on her echoing form;
more stirred by the whiff of her, dizzy with ale, his left arm walloping
over her waist, but missing and squeezing, more thrust than hug,
just under the breastbone he loves so her wrought silver denture
(three upper incisors avulsed in a fall from a horse and hitherto
schtum) wings forth on that sudden upshot of air, abrupt
as an utterance too long held, and rings on the earthenware pitcher,
hic hic, her rhythm disrupting before her breath settles
and young Mrs Heimlich recovers the gist of her dream.

The Hyacinth Under The Stairs

My father is wearing a hat, a grey hat; this much I know to be true.
One of those hats worn by Seventies salesmen, grey with a narrowish
brim, a front-to-back dent in the top, a band with a bit of sheen in
a similar colour. When it's not on his head it hangs on a hook, high
up at the top of the hallstand. It being a Monday his shoes will be
buffed to a shine. We waken each Sunday to eight polished pairs
on the lino in front of the paraffin stove in the hall. It could be a
Tuesday but this much I do know: he sells frozen food for a living.
First Birds Eye (we're reared on fish fingers) and then some time
later he moves on to H.B. ice-cream.

This morning he's heading for Derry, a journey of forty-odd miles.
He'll pop in on his customers as he goes by, take orders, ensure that
their freezers are full, and he'll stop at the pool in Strabane for his
mid-morning swim.

My father has had a long day and he's on his last call. Already he's
hungry and thinking of dinner at home. He's in a wee shop in the
Bogside, it's gone half past four, when the old lady owner, named Mrs
McCann, says "Jesus Christ Jimmy, you're fucked." He stares at her
then; he's known her this years; he's never heard her swear like this
before. She motions, the slightest of sideways nods, outside where the
brand-new Avenger is parked. It's a brassy gold colour that none of us
like. We long for our old red Cortina estate; my wee brother Joseph
who sits up in front on the handbrake complains the Avenger's is
thinner, sticks into his bum, despite the red cushion my mother has
made. She calls it his saddle and teaches him 'Home on the Range'.

My father been filling an order, head down, but he straightens
up now and turns round. Through the mesh on the window, he
makes out two men with their hoods up. They're both wearing
balaclavas, and sunglasses too. A still of my father before he steps
outside. He's played here by Elvis Costello.

It's raining, it's snowing, it's the hottest day of the hottest summer on record for fifteen years. My father frisks his pockets. Unable to find his Reactolites, he steps out into the glare. He squints towards the Avenger, his right hand shielding his eyes. A thick Derry accent, the taller man shouts:

"Mister, is this your car?"

"It is, aye."

"We need it."

My father is cool as a choc-ice or frozen fish:

"Not as badly as I do lads," the sales course on empathy coming in handy, "I've a job to do too, I've a wife and six children expecting me home, could youse not find somebody else's car to lift."

The other young man looks twitchy, he's standing a yard from my Da. When my father smells sweet sticky sickening fear, he assumes that the reek is his own. But then it moves closer, a slow sideways step like a crab. Your man's side to side with him now, and slightly behind. His right hand is deep in his anorak pocket; he presses against my Dad.

"I've stuff in the car for my work, can youse help me?" (This is the second time Daddy's said youse – we're skelped if we say that at home.) The frightened man pushes him harder, he jabs at Dad's ribs. The other one sighs but comes over to Dad, and together they start to unload, while the one with his hand in his pocket stands stiff as a palace guard. My Dad sees him trying to light a match with one hand, and he stifles a smile as he spills them all over the ground. The heads of his Swan Vesta matches a red dot-to-dot.

The boxes they shift contain posters, stickers for freezers, incentives for soon-to-be stockists, rewards for the loyal, additional order books. It takes them two trips to completely shift the pruck. My father remembers his manners, says thanks to the man, rips open a box, and hands him a couple of packets of felt-tip pens, T-shirts with Captain Birds Eye on the front, a couple of *Come Home to Birds Eye Country* mugs. Handing over the keys to his company car, he remembers the black leather grip with his wet swimming gear. The grip was his Dad's; he retrieves it before they drive off. I picture him frozen there clutching his bag, watching his car disappear through the heat haze, the blizzard, a boy who has missed the last bus.

May McCann has wet tea but my father now craves something stronger. He asks can he use her phone and goes out to the hall where he calls an acquaintance, Pat Boyle, a doctor in Derry who went to the College of Surgeons with Uncle John. He reminds my father to phone the police – the insurance people will need a detailed report. My father thanks Mrs Mc Cann who refuses point blank to take cash for the call. The shop suddenly fills and she tells him to put his stuff out the back and to leave through the hall when he's done. As he does so he passes the telephone table, and he slides a shiny new ten pence piece just under the telephone book.

My father meets Pat in the pub he suggests, not far from Mrs Mc's shop. He's the one pint of Guinness, a brandy for shock, or that's what he says to my Mum. "Look into the car-park for us, will you, Jimmy." There are four or five beat-looking cars, a sore thumb among them the sheen of the brassy Avenger, its come-and-get-me English registration. Wee Joseph's red cushion's been tossed on the parcel shelf. Pat Boyle's stony-faced as my Dad scans the bar. "Now, Jimmy, just finish your drinks. You'll come back to the house and we'll get you a taxi to Omagh."

When my father arrives two hours late for his dinner, he slurs. Our mother's been pacing the room. "Your tea's in the oven, it's ruined, sit down, for God's sake, and have something to eat."

She goes out to the scullery, banging the door but he follows, she shouts then they whisper, she sends us up early to bed with our homework half-done. Myself and my sister tiptoe back down and we listen a while at the door. They're still talking low and we hear 'balaclava' and 'young', and when Sheila hears 'gun' she coughs and my mother comes out. She chases us back to our beds where we whisper and dream.

My father wore a hat when I was little
we lived in Omagh O-M-A-G-Haitch or –Aitch
as tribally decreed. He was a travelling salesman
for ice-cream; a Dublin firm Hughes Brothers or H.B.
he was their Northern Ireland diplomat.

He knew his clients well – a studied discipline,
some would not buy HB ice-cream on principle.
My father'd done his homework;
to some he'd sell Haitch
B, to others Aitch B.

One day in Derry/Londonderry my father's car was hijacked.
The men wore hats pulled down with holes for eyes and mouth,
They held a gun, they nudged his hat,
They asked my father where we lived
And ordered him to spell it.

I'd honestly thought that this version was true. When I find out it
didn't quite happen like that I am gutted; I feel that I've let people
down. I can only suppose that I pieced it together from whispers,
and dreamt up the rest in the silence which fell on that day.

But silence is not a deep-freeze. A silence breeds stories, like hyacinths
under the stairs. Secrecy's soil for their roots, but for flowering they
need warmth and light. My father's surprised when the poem is
published and tells me what actually happened. Or I should say his
version, refracted through memory's prism, and time, and the love of a
story, well-told. He can neither refute nor corroborate anything now.

But that isn't ever the end; there is always at least the one postscript,
perhaps if we're lucky a joke. The next day my father remembers his
shades. He needs them for driving, Dr Scott made them up to my
father's prescription, they cost him an arm and a leg, and they're
bugger-all use, he says, to anyone else. He reckons they're in the glove
compartment of the stolen car. He phones up Pat Boyle. Postmarked

Londonderry, by Friday the glasses return to my father by way of Her Majesty's mail.

The Chrysler Avenger is found, burnt out on a housing estate. A shiny new pillar-box red Ford Cortina estate is delivered the following week.

Fathom

... the furthest distances I've travelled
have been those between people
 – Leontia Flynn

1. Father
(at the Forty-foot Gentlemen's Bathing Place)

Seven thirty a.m.
and I love that men
are different
when wet.

We're sea-changed,
leagues of seals,
rasping, clapping,
rapturing the air.

I'm glad the water's cold.
And though my father
taught me everything

I know about salt water,
for fifty weeks per annum
he remained arms' length inland.

2. *Farther*

Not necessarily needing to know
I launch into these buoyant
introductions: 'Hey Dad, it's Paula,
your favourite daughter your

beautiful blow-in from Belfast,'
my mother priming him well
in advance, so that I'm a little
deflated but hardly surprised

when he risks 'Are you married
to one of my sons?' 'Father,'
I breeze 'Bishop Hegarty'd never

agree.' And his smile as he fathoms
the quip soon sinks, repeating
how terribly terribly sorry he is.

3. Further

Close to the close of your life, you wash up
in a strange house with a woman old enough
to be your mother insisting she is your wife.
Despite your rebuttals she's wedded to her lies.

You try the doors, her ladyship has them locked.
You spot your father's shooting-stick,
you've really got to fly, you say, and put
a window in. Next thing you la-la-la-

land in some class of hotel where the women
are very much younger with lovely hands;
the exits here, you swiftly establish, are shut

with a hush-hush code. You've stashed the stick
and smash a panel in. They belt you in a comfy chair,
to anchor you, they say, and call you 'pet'.

4. *Faster*

I don't think I ever married, did I? This
at the buzz-locked doors as I'm heading, the same day
he's quizzed me how long this interment (sic) will last.
You did Dad, the Star of the County you claimed.

He grins. And I've more to report. Go on.
She bore you six children. Away. It's true.
Would you like me to introduce you to one?
I would. God. That would be great.

Well, Father. We shake.
It's a pleasure to meet you.
He beams.

When I leave I am borne
on the keen conviction
he liked me.

5. *Falter*

Our father one ankle in Heaven
trouser-leg rolled to the knee –
your time not come – the other one
stuck as it is and swollen.

There is yet time in this dry hotel,
as your wide straddle falters the tide recedes
til your greeting's a watery smile you float
for the flickering hosts of the faces you meet,

above whose static you tune to the sirens –
song with your name on –
now well within range;

though embracing's beyond us
I'd sing to deliver you
home for the last how long

Notice

The swimmer eschews
all manner of insulation.
Observation is not
forbidden, though may

give rise to stiffness,
frostbite, or both.
Observers should remain
outwith the perimeter;

numbers are strictly
restricted to two or three.
Observers do so wholly
at their own risk.

Cajoling is not permitted.
It precipitates even
more protracted delays.
Observers should desist

from holding their breath
while the swimmer is under.
The swimmer will dive
only once. No-one

may photograph
the moment of entry.
On no condition
must anyone touch

the swimmer.
After she plunges
up you can whoop
your lungs out,

petrify the gulls.

A Ribbon for Anne Mc Alarney
Newcastle County Down, July 12 2012

You tender these: one
warm hen's egg in freckled fawn
(I'd thought them brown
til then); a small round spirit
level – a bubble-drum in lurid Red
Hand red; a pencil sharpener, dull
metallic grey.
                    Your after-
thought a single pencil paring,
a brittle fan whose fluted band's
a glinting wave of *W*s in blue.
        For you, my friend,
a ribbon in whatever hue
you're choosing. This.

Notes on the Poems

In 'Finding the Well' the *lump on my hand* would have been a ganglion cyst. The medical wisdom, now outdated, was to rupture the cyst by striking it with a heavy book. The favoured text was a bible; for this reason it was also known as a Bible or Gideon cyst.

'A Dog Called Chance' was written on 29 August 1998, two weeks after the Omagh bomb which, on August 15th that year, killed 29 people including a woman pregnant with twins.

In 'Seeing Things', Winter Park Colorado is home to the U.S. National Ski Centre for the Disabled.

In 'The Birds of Sri Lanka' sequence, the first two sections were written before, and the final sections following, the Indian Ocean Tsunami of December 26th 2004.

Permissions

The opening quotations are from Stuart Dybek's poem 'Anti-Memoir' in his collection *Streets in Their Own Ink* (Farrar, Straus and Giroux, 2004), and Robert Hayden's poem 'Those Winter Sundays' in *Collected Poems of Robert Hayden* (Liveright Publishing Corporation, 1985)

The quotation which opens the poem 'Fathom' on page 60 is from Leontia Flynn's poem 'The furthest distances I've travelled' from *These Days* (Jonathan Cape, 2004)